HOW TO
PREVENT AND SAFELY
MANAGE PHYSICAL
AGGRESSION AND
PROPERTY DESTRUCTION

Gary Stephen Allison

HOW TO IMPROVE CLASSROOM BEHAVIOR SERIES

SERIES EDITORS

Saul Axelrod
Steven C. Mathews

pro·ed
An International Publisher

8700 Shoal Creek Boulevard
Austin, Texas 78757-6897
800/897-3202   Fax 800/397-7633
www.proedinc.com

© 2003 by PRO-ED, Inc.
8700 Shoal Creek Boulevard
Austin, Texas 78757-6897
800/897-3202   Fax 800/397-7633
www.proedinc.com

Library of Congress Cataloging-in-Publication Data

Allison, Gary Stephen.
      How to prevent and safely manage physical aggression and property destruction / Gary
Stephen Allison.
          p.   cm. — (How to improve classroom behavior series)
      Includes bibliographical references (p.).
      ISBN 0-89079-911-3
      1. Classroom management.   2. Behavior modification.   3. Aggressiveness.   4. School
vandalism—Prevention.   I. Title.   II. Series.

LB3013.A39   2003
371.7'82—dc21

                                                                        2002190832

This book is designed in Minion and Gill Sans.

Printed in the United States of America

1   2   3   4   5   6   7   8   9   10   06   05   04   03   02

CONTENTS

FOREWORD

Having spent several years as a classroom teacher, as a principal of both regular and special education students, and as an educational researcher, it has long been apparent to me that there is a need for materials that provide quick solutions to specific classroom problems. The *How To Improve Classroom Behavior Series* edited by Saul Axelrod and Steven C. Mathews fills that need. Although there have been a number of excellent research studies and texts that present effective classroom management techniques, the beauty of this series is that the authors have used their own experiences and surveyed the literature to present effective procedures that efficiently guide teachers toward solutions of common classroom management problems.

The value of such a series should be apparent. Teachers faced with particular problems, such as students who are disruptive or who bully or tease, can consult the series for solutions. Ideally these books will be found on a bookshelf in the teachers' lounge. Without having to search through professional journals or cumbersome texts, teachers will easily be able to focus on the particular behavior that is a topic of concern. Principals, school psychologists, counselors, and other professionals to whom teachers sometimes refer students with problem behaviors, will also find these texts useful in providing solutions for teachers. It also should prove extremely helpful, especially to beginning teachers, when a principal or psychologist can provide a simple, uncluttered text that tells the teacher exactly what to do in certain problem situations.

The booklets in the series are presented in such a way that they help the user to clearly define the behavior of concern and then to implement step-by-step programs that deal effectively with that behavior. Because the booklets are written in straightforward, nontechnical language, teachers will not become bogged down in trying to understand psychological jargon or complex procedures.

Saul Axelrod is a respected researcher and author. He has published more than 60 research articles and book chapters on behavior and eight books that deal with classroom problems. An excellent writer, he has served on the editorial boards of ten prominent psychological and educational journals. As a licensed psychologist and professor of special education, he has wide experience in instructing teachers in the use of classroom management techniques. Due to his extensive experience and many professional contacts, he and his coeditor were able to select authors well qualified to write each booklet in the series.

Steven C. Mathews is an educator who has spent over 30 years in educational publishing, including stints as managing editor of education for the College Division of Allyn & Bacon and as editor in chief of PRO-ED. He served two terms as president of the Austin, Texas, Chapter of the Council for Exceptional Children and has served on advisory committees for the American Speech-Language-Hearing Association, Council for Learning Disabilities, and Texas Council for Exceptional Children. His publications include tests and therapy materials.

It has been my privilege to work closely with both Saul and Steve. I participated with Saul in several of his first research publications and coauthored with him my most recent publication. I know firsthand that he is an excellent researcher, teacher, and author. I know of no one better qualified to produce this series. I have also worked closely with Steve, who served as managing editor for a number of my publications, including my own *How To Manage Behavior Series.* His skill in guiding the selection of topics and in shaping and polishing manuscripts is unparalleled in my experience. Their cooperative efforts make this series a valuable contribution to the field of teacher education.

R. Vance Hall
Professor Emeritus
University of Kansas

PREFACE TO SERIES

The idea for the *How To Improve Classroom Behavior Series* grew from our conversations with R. Vance Hall. His popular series of booklets called *How To Manage Behavior* presents, in a step-by-step manner, behavioral procedures and techniques. Although they are practical and quick to read, the booklets in his series do not easily show a teacher who may be unfamiliar with behavioral techniques which ones would be best to use in specific situations. We agreed that a new series was needed—a series that would present behavioral techniques in booklets that each address a specific problem behavior that teachers encounter in their classrooms.

Development of the Series

We first wanted to determine what common behavior problems occur in the classroom. In reviewing the literature (Bender, 1987; Bibou-Nakou, Kiosseoglou, & Stogiannidou, 2000; Bickerstaff, Leon, & Hudson, 1997; Elam, 1987, 1989; Elam, Rose, & Gallup, 1994; Fagen, 1986; Gibbons & Jones, 1994; Greenlee & Ogletree, 1993; Jones, Quah, & Charlton, 1996; Malone, Bonitz, & Rickett, 1998; Mastrilli & Brown, 1999; Ordover, 1997), we found that common classroom behavior problems were consistently reported regardless of the age of the student, the type of classroom, the special needs of the student, the experience of the teacher, the passage of time, or the part of the world. This review produced a preliminary list of possible topics for the series.

The preliminary list was then compared to topics presented in textbooks used in courses on behavior management and classroom discipline (e.g., Charles, 1999; Kaplan, 1995, 2000; Sloane, 1988; Walker & Walker, 1991; Workman & Katz, 1995). The list was also evaluated by educators and psychologists from university and other school settings. Their input helped us create a revised list of topics.

The final list of topics, reflected in the titles of the *How To Improve Classroom Behavior Series,* was created by combining topics that had common themes and eliminating topics that did not lend themselves to the format of the series. After the final list was completed, we contacted potential authors for each booklet. Each author selected has a background related to the topic, knowledge of current behavioral principles, and experience working directly with teachers and students.

Format of the Series

All the booklets in the series were written in the same format. Each booklet includes the following:

- Practical and nontechnical information
- All the information a teacher needs to implement a strategy
- Step-by-step strategy presentation
- Numerous strategy suggestions from which the reader can choose
- Numerous examples of various levels of problem severity, ages of students, and instructional settings
- Interactive learning procedures with space and prompts for the reader to make oral or written responses
- References and suggestions for further readings

Uses of the Series

Each of the booklets in the series may be used independently or in conjunction with the other booklets. Each can be read and the information used by regular classroom teachers, special education teachers, teachers in collaborative classrooms, school psychologists, and anyone else who has students who exhibit the behavior that is the topic of the booklet.

The design of the booklets allows them to be used without additional information. However, they also lend themselves to workshop, in-service, or consultation situations. They are ideal for a special education teacher, school psychologist, or other consultant to share with a teacher who requests information or who reports a problem in her or his classroom.

Acknowledgments

We would first like to thank our friend R. Vance Hall for his advice, counsel, and patience, and for his writing the foreword to the series. The series would not exist without Vance's contributions.

We would also like to thank the contributors to the series. They all have prepared manuscripts following a prescribed format in a very short period of time. The many people at PRO-ED who have contributed to the series from its inception through its publication also have earned our thanks and respect.

Saul Axelrod and
Steven C. Mathews
Series Editors

Series References

Bender, W. N. (1987). Correlates of classroom behavior problems among learning disabled and nondisabled children in mainstream classes. *Learning Disabilities Quarterly, 10,* 317–324.

Bibou-Nakou, I., Kiosseoglou, G., & Stogiannidou, A. (2000). Elementary teacher's perceptions regarding school behavior problems: Implications for school psychological services. *Psychology in the Schools, 37,* 123–134.

Bickerstaff, S., Leon, S. H., & Hudson, J. G. (1997). Preserving the opportunity for education: Texas' alternative education programs for disruptive youth. *Journal of Law and Education, 26,* 1–39.

Charles, C. M. (1999). *Building classroom discipline* (6th ed.). New York: Longman.

Elam, S. M. (1987). Differences between educators and the public on questions of education policy. *Phi Delta Kappan, 69,* 294–296.

Elam, S. M. (1989). The second Gallup/Phi Delta Kappa poll of teachers' attitudes toward the public schools. *Phi Delta Kappan, 70,* 785–798.

Elam, S. M., Rose, L. C., & Gallup, A. M. (1994). The 26th annual Phi Delta Kappa/Gallup poll of the public's attitude toward the public schools. *Phi Delta Kappan, 76,* 41–56.

Fagen, S. A. (1986). Least intensive interventions for classroom behavior problems. *Pointer, 31,* 21–28.

Gibbons, L., & Jones, L. (1994). Novice teachers' reflectivity upon their classroom management. (ERIC Documentation Reproduction Service No. ED386446)

Greenlee, A. R., & Ogletree, E. J. (1993). Teachers' attitude toward student discipline problems and classroom management strategies. (ERIC Documentation Reproduction Service No. ED364330)

Jones, K., Quah, M. L., & Charlton, T. (1996). Behaviour which primary and special school teachers in Singapore find most troublesome. *Research in Education, 55,* 62–73.

Kaplan, J. S. (1995). *Beyond behavior modification: A cognitive–behavioral approach to behavior management in the school* (3rd ed.). Austin, TX: PRO-ED.

Kaplan, J. S. (2000). *Beyond functional assessment: A social–cognitive approach to the evaluation of behavior problems in children and youth.* Austin, TX: PRO-ED.

Malone, B. G., Bonitz, D. A., & Rickett, M. M. (1998). Teacher perceptions of disruptive behavior: Maintaining instructional focus. *Educational Horizons, 76,* 189–194.

Mastrilli, T. M., & Brown, D. S. (1999). Elementary student teachers' cases: An analysis of dilemmas and solutions. *Action in Teacher Education, 21,* 50–60.

Ordover, E. (1997). *Inclusion of students with disabilities who are labled "disruptive": Issues papers for legal advocates and parents.* Boston: Center for Law and Education.

Sloane, H. N. (1988). *The good kid book: How to solve the 16 most common behavior problems.* Champaign, IL: Research Press.

Walker, H. M., & Walker, J. E. (1991). *Coping with noncompliance in the classroom: A positive approach for teachers.* Austin, TX: PRO-ED.

Workman, E. A., & Katz, A. M. (1995). *Teaching behavioral self-control to students* (2nd ed.). Austin, TX: PRO-ED.

How To Improve Classroom Behavior Series

How To Help Students Remain Seated

How To Deal Effectively with Lying, Stealing, and Cheating

How To Prevent and Safely Manage Physical Aggression and Property Destruction

How To Help Students Complete Classwork and Homework Assignments

How To Help Students Play and Work Together

How To Deal with Students Who Challenge and Defy Authority

How To Deal Effectively with Whining and Tantrum Behaviors

How To Help Students Follow Directions, Pay Attention, and Stay on Task

Introduction

The student is in his seat, staring out the window. He suddenly throws his books against the wall, and now is approaching you in a threatening manner with his fists clenched at his side. This has all transpired in about 3 seconds. You did not anticipate this happening, and now all you have time to do is react. What do you do?

Have you ever taught students who were physically aggressive toward others and also destroyed property? Has a student ever attempted to (or succeeded in) punching you, kicking you, scratching you, pulling your hair, spitting on you, or throwing something at you? If this has ever happened to you, you are not alone. There are increasing references to "battered teacher syndrome" in the educational literature (Goldstein, Palumbo, Striepling, & Voutsinas, 1995), and teachers across the country are injured, sometimes severely, during student acting out episodes.

Remember those incidents in your career. Did you safely manage the situation? Was anyone injured? Did you know what to do? Did the other teachers come to your assistance? Chances are this was one of the most difficult, frightening, frustrating, and dangerous situations in your career. If you have a student engaging in physical aggression toward others and/or destroying property, you have a huge problem. If these behaviors occur on a regular basis, the problem is compounded and the chances of you or your students getting injured increase.

Teachers often do not feel prepared to deal with these very serious behaviors; therefore, the behaviors can cause disruption to the classroom (at the least) or serious injury to others. It has become apparent that it is not just students with disabilities or emotional/behavioral disorders who engage in these health- and life-threatening responses, but that they may be evident in any student population.

In the following pages are procedures, protocols, and approaches that teachers may find useful in preventing, safely managing, and most importantly, teaching alternatives to these dangerous behaviors.

Nature and Scope of Problem

There is no doubt that violence occurs in school settings. Violence in schools has received recent media attention, most probably due to recent shootings in schools across the country. Although these horrific events are relatively rare, incidents of aggression by students toward peers and teachers do occur with an alarming frequency (Leff, Power, & Manz, 2001). Sprague and Walker (2000) report that over 100,000 students bring weapons to school each day, and more than 40 students are killed or wounded with these weapons annually. They also report that more than 6,000 teachers are threatened annually, and well over 200 are physically injured by students on school grounds.

Due to this alarming trend, antisocial behavior, youth violence, and student safety are seen as huge concerns in American education and also in society at large. The Office of Juvenile Justice and Delinquency Prevention reports that the U.S. juvenile (all children ages 10–17) homicide rate has doubled in just 7 years (1993–2000). It also estimates that this U.S. juvenile population will double in the next decade and that the number of juvenile arrests for violent crime will double by the year 2010 (Sprague & Walker, 2000). There is also evidence that well-developed antisocial, aggressive behaviors that are evident early in a child's life are an accurate predictor of delinquency and violent behavior years later (Fagan, 1996; Loeber & Farrington, 1998). Given the current state of affairs, the problem of aggressive behavior by students in schools is real and must be addressed.

Behavior Intervention Plans

Selecting the Target Behavior

Physical aggression and property destruction are usually not that difficult to operationally define. The specific actions that constitute episodes of these behaviors usually make up health- or life-threatening situations that teachers are intimately familiar with. The responses that are the most seriously threatening to life or health should be selected and intervened with first. You must also consider whether the behaviors in question have been selected in a logical order. Thinking in terms of desirable, necessary, and urgent criteria may be helpful in the selection and prioritization of the target behaviors. There are some behaviors that may be *desirable* to change (e.g., infrequent note passing or goofing off in class), but these behaviors may not be *necessary* to change. In other words, the behaviors may be desirable to change from the teacher's perspective because they are annoying on occasion, but they do not interfere with the act of teaching, nor do they negatively impact other students' ability to learn. A target behavior must be both *desirable* and *necessary* to change in order to be addressed formally with a behavior intervention plan. The behaviors must negatively impact the act of teaching or other students' ability to learn, be physically or psychologically unsafe to the student or peers, or be destructive of property (including theft) to be considered necessary or urgent to change. The last criterion, *urgent*, refers to behaviors that are severely threatening to health or life. This category includes physical aggression or property destruction that is so severe or chronic that it is considered to be a clear and present danger to the health and lives of others. Physical aggression and property destruction are almost always necessary and urgent to address.

Question 1

Target a behavior for change in a classroom, and give a rationale for the behavior you have chosen being at least desirable and necessary to change.

_____

_____

_____

_____

_____

_____

_____

_____

_____

Operationally Defining the Behavior: IBSOM

Once you have selected the target behavior (it is, at the least, desirable and necessary to change), you are now ready to operationally define it. The first question to ask: Is the behavior specific, observable, and measurable (IBSOM)? Can you describe in writing and orally the specific actions you have observed that constitute the behavior? Can the behavior be measured in some way? Counted? The operational definition is the written statement of what the behavior "looks like." It should be concise and use words that describe directly observable actions such as "kicks with right foot," "hits top of surfaces with closed right fist," or "grabs hair from behind with both hands with severe force." The operational definition should be familiar to and understood by all persons in the student's learning environment.

Question 2

Operationally define physical aggression or property destruction for one of your students.

_____

_____

_____

_____

Question 3

> Is your operational definition IBSOM? Would you be able to collect data using this definition?

_____

_____

Baseline Measures and Reflections on the Results

The next step is to get a baseline measure of the behaviors. This consists of a measure of the aggression or property destruction before a behavior intervention plan is developed and implemented. Due to the severity and danger of some situations, it is not always possible to obtain several days of baseline data. Other situations lend themselves to creating a baseline measure via incident reports and student discipline referral forms. Regardless of the situation, a baseline measure of the aggression or destruction is very important for measuring the effect of the soon-to-be implemented behavior intervention plan.

Once the data have been collected, they should be presented to the team (the primary teacher and all other staff involved with the student) in graphic form to allow for a visual analysis. The overriding reason for presenting data in graphic form is that "a picture is worth a thousand words" (Alberto & Troutman, 1999). In order to show a trend, there need to be at least three data points heading in the same direction. The team can then see if the behavior is ascending (increasing), descending (going down), stable (at a consistent rate), or variable (no clear pattern). If there are not enough data points available, the team at the least has a starting point for the intervention (e.g, there were three aggressions yesterday). It is crucial to know where the student is before you can tell where he or she is going; you must know how much of the behavior is actually occurring before you know how much it has changed.

It is also important to reflect on the baseline results and use the baseline as the starting point for changing behavior. Baseline measures can also yield helpful information such as the time of day that the behavior usually occurs, the most likely activities or tasks during which the aggression or destruction occurs, or even the staff most likely to encounter aggression or destruction with the student.

Accurate and ongoing data collection will enable you to see the extent of the problem, the effects of your behavior intervention plan, and the results of any changes to the plan. An example of a baseline measure is shown in Figure 1.

Questions

4. Is the baseline in Figure 1 stable, variable, ascending, or descending?

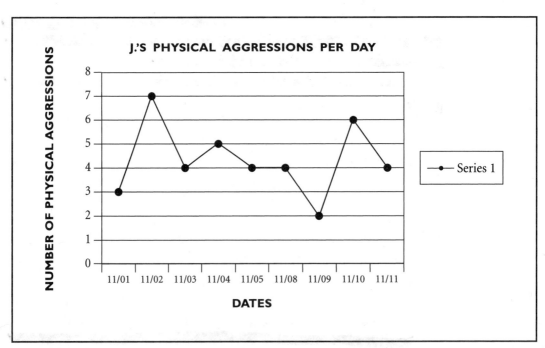

Figure 1. The number of physical aggressions, shown as part of a baseline measure.

5. Is there any trend in evidence?

_____

6. What is the average number of aggressions per day for student J.?

_____

7. What are your reflections on this baseline?

_____

_____

_____

_____

_____

Functional Assessment and Analysis

Once a behavior has been selected, defined, and measured, it is time to perform at least a brief functional assessment and analysis. Functional assessment involves direct observations of students in natural environments, and rules out with some confidence medical factors, diet, epilepsy, and other variables that may be causing the behavior of concern. Functional analysis involves manipulation of conditions to validate or invalidate the hypothesis of what causes the behavior and what maintains the behavior (Alberto & Troutman, 1999; Zirpoli & Melloy, 1997).

There are many commercially available behavior rating scales and observational recording devices that can be used in a functional assessment. It is obviously very important to rule out seizure activity, sleep deprivation, or other biological variables that may be presenting as aggressive or destructive behavior. There are also some ethical and legal issues involved in functional analysis procedures that might make the aggresive behavior happen during manipulation of conditions. An example might be a student who engages in intense aggressive and destructive behavior. Do you *want* to make this behavior occur during the functional assessment and analysis? If the student or peers are injured during a functional analysis procedure, it might be difficult for the teacher to defend the actions that caused the behavior in the first place.

If the teacher can rule out some confounding factors with at least moderate confidence and make a very educated guess as to what is making the aggressive or destructive behavior happen and what is maintaining the behavior, this information can help produce a correct behavior intervention plan.

Some typical things that "make behavior happen" according to a functional assessment include conditions of low attention, high demands, restricted access (student told "no" or "wait"; a desirable object is visible, but unreachable), or low stimulation. Some typical variables that might make aggressive behavior keep happening include attention, escape, stimulation, access to tangible items, and countercontrol (e.g., the student who tries to counter every move the teacher makes in an attempt to disrupt the class or gain control).

Regardless of the teacher's findings, the functional assessment is the guide to selecting the correct and most effective behavior intervention plan. The teacher's functional prescription is based on the findings actually telling him or her what to do as far as the intervention. One example is if a student appears to be aggressive toward the teacher mostly during conditions of low attention, in an attempt to gain the teacher's attention, then the prescription would be to change the low attention condition. Teaching the student a better way to get teacher attention (maybe hand raising) and giving abundant attention every time (initially) that the student performs the new behavior are also parts of the prescription. The last part of the prescription is to have a reactive strategy in case the aggression keeps happening, which it probably will until the new behavior gains dominance in the student's repertoire.

The functional assessment will direct the teacher as to which entry points to address in the behavior intervention plan. Please refer to the section on entry points for changing behavior.

Implementation of Behavior Intervention Plan and Monitoring

Now it is time to implement the behavior intervention plan. It is also important at this stage to train all staff who will be implementing the plan. It is equally important to train the student for whom the plan is designed to alert him or her to both the positive components as well as the reactive components. An example would be informing the student of the privileges and other rewards she can earn in the program and also the consequences for the physical aggression or property destruction. Group training sessions involving all persons who will be working with the student are usually helpful as well as some individual sessions. Follow-up to maintain program integrity and to prevent program "drift" and program "anarchy" is a very important consideration at this time. Program integrity is what a teacher wishes to achieve with the behavior intervention plan. It is defined as all involved staff implementing the plan accurately and consistently. Maintaining program integrity will help prevent program drift, which may occur when all staff are not implementing the plan consistently, and some staff are beginning to drift and put their own twist on the plan. If you do not monitor the implementation of your behavior intervention plan carefully and thoroughly, you may encounter program anarchy in which staff are implementing a plan so different from the original that it is hard to recognize. The program integrity, program drift, and program anarchy paradigm is functional because if the follow-up catches the program at the drift stage, it is usually fairly easy to get the staff back to program integrity. It should be noted that if the program reaches the anarchy stage, it is sometimes very difficult to get back to program integrity; therefore, follow-up and monitoring are crucial to maintaining program integrity.

Question 8

> What would you do if program drift became evident in your classroom with a new behavior intervention program? What could you do immediately to prevent program anarchy?

_____

_____

_____

_____

_____

_____

_____

_____

_____

The Instructional Cycle, Reflections, and Revisions to Behavior Intervention Plan

Another part of follow-up and monitoring is making program revisions as the program progresses—a "fine-tuning" approach. Often, the initial program approach needs some subtle changes to best address the needs of the student. On occasion, the program will require a major overhaul when it proves to be ineffective in changing the aggressive behaviors. Changes to the program are best done in a team context. Everyone who has any kind of contact with the student is a member of the team and should be informed immediately of any program changes. The team would also include school administration, the family, and all other concerned and involved persons.

Changes to the program should be data-based decisions. Looking at the data, after the baseline measure, during the first phase of the new program will yield very useful information. Is the aggressive behavior decreasing? Is it increasing? Or is there no change? Based on a visual analysis of the program implementation data, the teacher will decide whether to make changes to the program. If there is an increase in incidents of aggressive behavior, there is obviously something wrong and it may be the program itself. The program might be inadvertently reinforcing aggression; the reinforcers might not be powerful enough; there might be problems with implementation; there might be competing contingencies in the environment. A thorough inspection of the program, the environment, the staff implementing the program, and other possible confounding variables is advised if there is no reduction in the aggressive behaviors after a reasonable amount of time. Typically, after a week to 10 days, the program should have some effect on the level of aggression or destruction.

The instructional cycle is a functional way to look at the intervention and monitoring of a behavior intervention plan. The cycle is assess–reflect–devise–implement–reflect–monitor–reflect and then back to assess, and so on. It is a continuous loop by which teachers continuously assess the student, reflect on the results of the assessment, devise a plan based on the assessment, implement the plan, reflect on the implementation, monitor results, reflect, then re-assess whether the plan is effective. With behavior intervention plans, this cycle is easy to follow and very effective. Assess using the baseline and other measures; reflect on the results; devise a plan; implement the plan; reflect on the plan (is it working?); then continuously monitor the results and re-assess at regular intervals. It is crucial to follow this cycle to maintain program integrity, to make changes when necessary, and to best support the behavior change in the student.

Documentation is always important in changing behavior in a student who has excess aggression or who destroys property. Ongoing data collection is essential to measure the impact of the behavior intervention plan on the student's rate of aggressive behavior. Some different topographies (forms) of aggressive behavior may be important to analyze when assessing the impact of the program on the student's behavior. It may be that the rate of the aggressive behavior is key. The number of occurrences of the behavior in question may be the single most important measure. If the program has produced a sustained decrease, the program is likely a success. Just as important in some cases is the duration of the episodes of aggressive behavior. A student may engage in few episodes of aggressive behavior per day or week, but each episode might last 15 to 20 minutes before the student calms. In this case, duration is a measure of behavior that should be taken into account. A teacher once told me that a student who was exhibiting out-of-seat behavior in her classroom had just had a great day because he "only had one incident of the out-of-seat behavior the whole school day." When asked how long the episode of out of seat had lasted, she said, "Well, about 4 hours." Obviously in this case the duration of the behavior was as important to measure as the frequency of the behavior.

Question 9

Name three forms of current data collection in your classroom and describe how they are used. If you do not currently collect behavior data, suggest three forms that might work for you.

a. _____

_____

b. _____

_____

c. _____

_____

Documentation is crucial in educational settings. It is the lasting record of a student's behavior as well as a teacher's first line of defense in a worst-case scenario of litigation. I often tell my teachers in training that "If it is not written down, it did not happen," meaning that they have to document their activities and student outcomes.

Question 10

Ariel, a student in your classroom, has been presenting aggressive behavior in the form of punching classmates with a closed fist with moderate force. She averages 4.5 incidents per school day, and the new behavior intervention program has reduced this rate to an average of 2.0 incidents per school day after a full week of implementation.

> Is your program a success? Why or why not? What other information do you need to decide?

_____

_____

_____

_____

_____

_____

_____

_____

Putting It All Together in Your Classroom

Now that you have completed this section, it is time to put all this information to work in your classroom. The flow of events in your classroom is depicted in Figure 2. As you complete the various activities and tasks

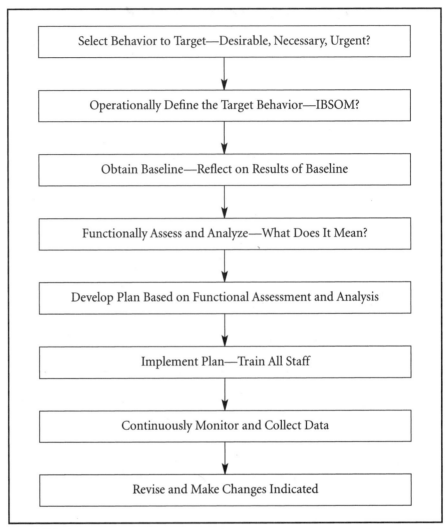

Figure 2. A flow chart for selecting, measuring, analyzing, and intervening in aggressive behavior in the classroom.

involved in the assessment and initial implementation phase, it may help you to reflect on the desired result of the behavior intervention plan. What is it that you would like the student to do instead of the aggressive behavior? Is the student capable of performing the new behavior that is being taught in the behavior intervention plan? What is the prognosis for the plan? Can the plan be implemented consistently in the various environments that the student is in on a daily basis? Are all staff trained in the plan, and is there a follow-up plan for ongoing monitoring of the student and the plan?

Proactive Strategies: Teaching Students What To Do, Rather Than Attempting To Teach Them What Not To Do

I always tell my undergraduate teaching candidates, "It is more effective to teach your students what to do, rather than attempting to teach them what not to do." What this means in this context is that you should be teaching your students other constructive responses, rather than just trying to teach them to "not be aggressive," or "don't hit," and so on. Part of the proactive approach to aggressive behavior is this teaching of what to do, rather than of what not to do.

There are basically two means of dealing with aggressive behavior in your classroom—proactive and reactive. Reactive strategies are addressed in a later section. This section offers some proactive, preventive strategies to use in your classroom that may enable you to prevent some aggressive behavior before it actually occurs.

Behavior is lawful, in the sense that it follows certain laws and is predictable in some situations. Something in the environment makes behavior happen and something also keeps it happening. Basically, if there is not something making the behavior happen and something that is keeping it happening, it simply does not occur. There is usually something in the environment that makes aggressive or destructive behavior happen, such as the student not getting enough attention, a room that is too noisy, or the like. There is also usually something in the environment that is maintaining the behavior, such as teacher or peer attention, the student escaping tasks or situations, and so on. Essentially, behavior can do only two things. First, it can add something pleasant to the environment, such as a compliment for prosocial behavior. Or, it can remove something unpleasant from the environment, such as a homework pass for a day without an aggressive incident.

Question 11

For one of your students, identify one thing that seems to make his or her aggressive behavior happen in the classroom and one thing that seems to keep the behavior happening.

_____

_____

_____

_____

_____

Antecedent Teaching: Entry Point #1 for Behavior Change and Support

Antecedents are an excellent place to start to prevent aggressive behavior in your classroom and can be considered entry point #1 for changing behavior. This is the part of teaching that sets the stage for student behavior to occur. Antecedent teaching involves using everything from classroom rules, routines, schedules, and so on, to the actual physical layout of the classroom. A well-run classroom has a comfortable (not boring), reliable, and predictable schedule, clear academic and non-academic routines, and clear expectations for behavior. Classroom rules are a great way to make more concrete your expectations for your students' behavior. Classroom rules should be posted and taught like any other lesson. A wonderful opening day activity in any classroom is developing the classroom rules with the students. This activity can make the students vested in the rules and, therefore, more apt to follow them. Posting the rules enables a teacher to refer to them as needed, and can also be a visual cue for the students' appropriate behavior. Rules should be phrased positively in terms of what students should do, as opposed to just listing behavioral prohibitions. I have seen classroom rules that resemble commandments—thou shalt not do this, this, that, and you better not do that either. If you phrase your classroom rules in terms of what students should do, however, more prosocial behaviors in your students will probably be the result.

Other components of entry point #1 include the comfort level of the classroom (e.g., temperature, seating arrangement, noise level), the level of stimulation, and teacher–student interactions. The temperature should be comfortable (i.e., not too hot, not too cold). I have been in adjacent classrooms where it was so cold in one room you could "hang meat in there" and in the next one it was so warm you could "cure meat in there." The seats should be at least relatively comfortable. The noise level should be appropriate for the current activity (e.g., quiet for independent seatwork), and the level of stimulation should be appropriate for the present group of students. Part of level of stimulation is chromesics—the study of the impact of color and stimulation on human behavior. Chromesics are used all around us, as evidenced by fast-food establishments using bright oranges, yellows, and so on, and fine dining establishments using subdued lighting and more earth tones, deep reds, and so on. The reasons for the use of these colors are that fast-food establishments want you to eat and leave, whereas fine dining establishments prefer you to stay longer and spend more money. The last part of entry point #1 is teacher–student interactions. Teachers should treat students with dignity and respect, regardless of their behavior. Typically, when you treat students with dignity and respect that is what you receive in return.

The research at this point tells us that students learn best when their basic needs are met (e.g., food, clothing, shelter), they are relatively comfortable, and they are at least somewhat motivated to learn. Teachers should examine and reflect on their classroom in terms of entry point #1, because it is extremely effective for changing behavior.

Question 12

Critique your classroom in terms of entry point #1. What areas do you see as strengths? What areas need improvement, and how will you improve them?

_____

_____

_____

_____

_____

_____

_____

Entry Points #2, #3, and #4

Entry point #2 is called influencing emotional characteristics and deals with the emotional makeup of the student and how this may have an affect on the aggressive behavior that is occurring. This entry point is also a place to determine whether the behavior may be occurring as a symptom of something else (e.g., emotional disturbance or psychiatric problem) or whether the student can respond to certain approaches. If your student is very high-strung, you might want to take a more indirect approach to behavior; conversely, if your student is very calm for the most part, you may be able to be more direct. This entry point for changing behavior can also include family issues, the need for counseling or other nonbehavioral approaches, or possibly some undetected medical conditions that are contributing to the aggressive behavior.

Entry point #3 is the behavior itself and the teaching of a functional alternative or other competing response. Sometimes the best approach to changing behavior is to address the aggressive behavior itself and teach the student an alternative to that aggression. Teaching alternative responses is addressed in a later section.

Entry point #4 is called consequence manipulation. This is historically where teachers look first when trying to change aggressive behavior in their classrooms. The provision of consequences for both desired behavior and undesired behavior is always part of an effective behavior intervention program. Positive reinforcement for engaging in alternatives to aggressive behavior, naturally occurring consequences for aggressive behavior, and the teaching of alternatives to aggression are the bedrock of any effective behavior intervention plan.

Question 13

For one of your students who engages in aggressive or destructive behavior, name an approach for each entry point for behavior change that you could incorporate in your classroom.

_____

_____

_____

_____

_____

_____

_____

_____

_____

_____

The value of using entry points for behavior change is that a good behavior intervention plan addresses all four points, and that the teacher knows that not all entry points apply to each case but that they should be examined.

Question 14

How does your classroom affect student behavior? Name three specific ways in which a classroom can increase or decrease aggressive student behavior.

a. _____

_____

b. _____

_____

c. _____

_____

Teaching Functional Alternatives: Response Competition

Teaching functional alternatives is one of the most effective ways to change aggressive behavior in the classroom. There is almost always a behavior that can be taught to the student that will serve the same function as the aggressive behavior. If the teacher thinks about it, there should be a better way for this student to get what he or she wants, instead of engaging in aggressive behavior. If the functional assessment and analysis indicate that the student is engaging in the aggressive behavior to escape social and academic demands, could the student be taught to ask for short breaks? If the student is destroying property to gain teacher attention, could the student be taught to ask the teacher for attention? It appears that much of the aggressive behavior that we see in classrooms has communicative intent. The student may be communicating by behavior that "I am upset, I have a headache, I want a break," and so on. Sometimes effective communication is an excellent alternative response for students who engage in aggressive behavior. Students who have a limited communication repertoire sometimes engage in behaviors of concern in order to communicate their needs or wants.

If the teacher remembers that there is typically a functional alternative available that you can teach to the student, that it will serve the same function as the old aggressive or destructive behavior, and that this new behavior will actually be more effective for the student, then the teacher has just mastered this section!

Question 15

Name a functional alternative for a student who is chronically hitting his teacher to get his or her attention. How would you go about teaching this new behavior?

_____

_____

_____

_____

_____

_____

_____

_____

The way in which a behavior can gain dominance in a student's repertoire and replace the aggressive behavior is through response competition. In response competition there are two or more responses competing in the student's behavioral repertoire—aggression and communication, for example. A huge breakthrough happens when a student who has been aggressive toward you stops and begins to communicate instead. Another example is the student who begins to become agitated, then calms by going off by himself in the corner of the room for a few minutes. There are many responses in everyone's repertoire that are competing for dominance at any given time. A perfect example of response competition has to do with very young children (about 9 months to 1 year old) who have two main responses competing. Assuming a child has no physical disability, one of these responses gains dominance in that child's repertoire. Can you guess what the two behaviors are? They are crawling and walking. Walking will typically gain dominance. Why? Because it is quicker, more effective, and children get more attention for walking from caregivers and others. Now, this is exactly the same reason that new behaviors that we teach students to engage in besides aggressive behavior will gain dominance. They work better. They are quicker. They result in more reinforcement, and so forth.

Question 16

Suggest an alternative response, and describe how you would teach this alternative response for the following behaviors of concern.

a. Student hits peers to gain their attention.

_____

_____

_____

_____

_____

b. Student is aggressive toward you to gain your attention or to escape.

_____

_____

_____

_____

_____

c. Student destroys property and seems to be maintained by attention and the sound of the objects breaking.

_____

_____

_____

_____

_____

Differential Reinforcement: The 3:1 Rule

As we strive to have students engage in more prosocial, cooperative, and overall productive behaviors as opposed to aggressive behavior, it is extremely important to reinforce all incidents of engaging in the new alternative behavior. As I tell my undergraduate teaching students, "Pay attention to what you want to see more of in the future." In other words, the more you attend to a desirable behavior in your classroom, the more likely you are to see it in the future. Differential reinforcement, in its most basic sense, refers to reinforcing some behaviors and not reinforcing others. A part of the behavior intervention plan typically involves some type of formal and structured reinforcement schedule. As a teacher, paying attention to desirable behaviors in your classroom, both formally and informally, will almost certainly increase those responses.

A way for a teacher to ensure that desirable behaviors occur in her classroom is to follow the 3:1 rule. The 3:1 rule dictates that there should be approximately 3 affirmative feedbacks to students (e.g., "well done," "excellent," "beautiful work") to every 1 corrective feedback (e.g., "no," "wrong," "sit down"). The 3:1 rule does not mean that the teacher keeps an informal count in her head and thinks to herself, "Well, I just gave 3 affirmatives, time for 1 corrective!" It just means that at the end of the day your students should have heard about 3 times more affirmative than corrective feedback.

Sometimes student behaviors are so chronically inappropriate that it is difficult for teachers to find a behavior to praise. Teachers need to look for something desirable, however small, and pay attention to it. In my work with students with severe disabilities, I would often have trouble finding anything to praise because the students were engaging in stereotypic behavior and/or self-injurious behavior almost constantly. Nevertheless, I would look at them, think of a behavior that they were doing that was desirable, and say, "Good breathing." It was the only thing I could think of, but it gave me a start, and before I knew it other behaviors became noticeable and praiseworthy. If you ever have trouble finding something to praise in your students, or you do not quite believe that there is always something to praise, just remember "Good breathing."

Question 17

Name three behaviors by students in your classroom that you would praise and explain why you would praise these behaviors.

a. _____

_____

_____

_____

b. _____

_____

c. _____

Behavior Contracting

An effective approach to changing aggressive behavior is contracting, wherein the teacher and the student develop an agreement in writing. It is also a good practice to have both the teacher and the student sign the contract to formalize the agreement that the student will try to perform the new alternative behavior for a specified amount of time. Behavior contracts are contingencies that are formalized in writing. They may read "I, _____, agree to _____, in order to earn _____." It is always a good idea to have the student involved in the whole contracting procedure. Behavior contracts can also be used for gradual behavior reduction, reinforcement of alternative behaviors, agreement to abstain from aggression for a specified amount of time, and so forth.

The protocol that I use is one in which initially the teacher, the student, and I, as the behavior analyst, sit down and write the contract. Then we all (teacher, student, behavior analyst) sign the contract. Next, we all (if possible) proceed to the copy machine and make two copies. The student gets the original, and the teacher and behavior analyst each get a copy. This increases accountability.

I once worked with a student who lived in a group home arrangement and attended a private school for students with emotional and behavioral disorders. His aggression was intense and frequent. We implemented behavior contracting after the baseline measure was complete. We started with 15-minute verbal contracts. After he had some success using the alternative behaviors of exercise, communication, and coping strategies, we were able to very gradually increase the intervals of the contracts to a half hour, then an hour (at this point they became written contracts), then a half day, to a whole day, to every other day, and so on, while still providing stronger and stronger self-selected reinforcers. By the end of the program, this young man was working on 6-month contracts for sporting events, trips to the seashore, and the like. His behavior had dramatically improved, and he no longer was aggressive to others when agitated. Instead, he used his coping repertoire. It was my privilege to visit him a couple of years ago, and he wanted to show me something in his bedroom. After getting the okay from staff, we went into his room and on his wall was every single written contract we had ever signed. I had no idea that he had even kept them, but they obviously meant a lot to him! Life is full of contracts, and this approach approximates real life and can be extremely effective with many students.

Modeling Appropriate and Functional Behavior

Is it true that imitation is the sincerest form of flattery? Have you ever had a student imitate you? Was this mannerism flattering when you saw it being performed by the student? Students do observe teachers—how they look, how they dress, how they handle frustration, how they interact with other teachers, and virtually all other teacher behavior that they are witness to. Given that students observe teachers, it is important to use modeling as a technique in your classroom because you truly are a role model for your students, whether you want to be or not. As the teacher in the classroom, you can model the behaviors that you want your students to engage in, such as managing your anger, using coping skills, communicating instead of behaving aggressively, and so on. You should demonstrate the desired behaviors that you want to replace aggressive behavior on a regular basis in both formal and informal ways. You can run small group sessions using scenarios created by the students and have them explore alternatives to aggressive behavior. However, the most important source of this modeling is the daily behavior of the teacher in the classroom.

It makes sense that the more alternatives a student has to aggressive behavior, and the more the student actually sees these alternatives being demonstrated, the more likely the student is to actually use the alternatives. As a source of positive reinforcement and a model for students, you can affect their behavior and help to increase their prosocial, adaptive behavior repertoire.

Question 18

Name an alternative behavior for physical aggression or property destruction that you could teach a student, and write a behavior contract for the new behavior.

_____

_____

_____

_____

_____

_____

_____

_____

_____

_____

Reactive Strategies, or What To Do When Things Go Wrong

Crisis Prevention, Intervention, and Postvention

Students can act out verbally (e.g., profanity, screaming, yelling) or physically (aggression, self-injury, property destruction). This section concerns the physical acting out—physical aggression and property destruction. Teachers understand that students (and teachers) can be injured during physical aggression episodes and also that during the act of destroying property a student can injure himself or others (e.g., innocent bystanders being hit by flying objects).

Reactive strategies are used when a student is actually engaging in the aggressive or destructive behavior(s). The reactive strategies are the teacher's responses to these behaviors. If a student is physically aggressive toward you or a peer and/or is destroying property, your overriding concern becomes safety for your students and yourself. When a student's behavior has escalated to the point where he or she is a clear and present danger to self or others, it is time to intervene for safety.

Crisis development tends to give teachers at least a little time to verbally manage the situation. This is preferable to having to physically manage the situation. If a teacher has to physically manage an aggressive episode, it increases the risk of injury to the teacher, the student, and others. A literal hands-on approach to managing an aggressive incident should be an absolute last resort, although there are some situations that do require physical interventions for safety. It is important to note in these situations, that all precautions are observed and that restraint is implemented for safety and safety only, and not used as a punisher. The real key in crisis prevention is intervening early enough in crisis development to prevent further escalation of the behavior, that is, intervene when the behavior is escalating, not when it has already reached the point of no return. Figure 3 illustrates the model of crisis development and the appropriate teacher response at each stage.

Research shows that the vast majority of students do exhibit antecedent behaviors to a crisis, and this is where teachers need to intervene first—"catch it low, to prevent it high" (Goldstein et al., 1995). There is usually a clear escalation of behavior leading to physical aggression or property destruction, and if teachers can verbally intervene while the student is still in the early stages of crisis development, their chances for successfully de-escalating the situation are greatly enhanced.

Teachers should also be aware that sometimes these antecedent behaviors to crisis (observable behaviors that the student engages in

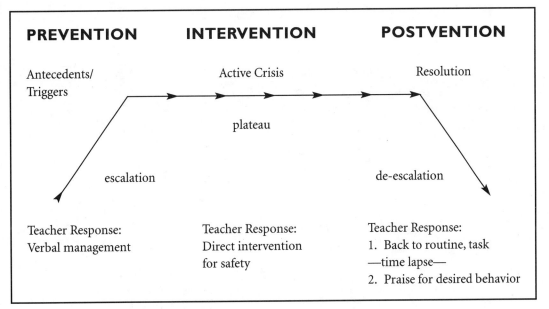

Figure 3. Crisis development and appropriate teacher response at each stage.

just prior to physically acting out) are very subtle and can be missed. An example is a student with whom I worked who would very lightly tap his foot just prior to assaulting others. If you did not notice the foot tapping and begin verbal management immediately, you would almost certainly encounter an all-out assault consisting of punching, kicking, scratching, and so on. Antecedent behaviors to crisis can also be very blatant and hard to miss. Another example is a young man with whom I worked who had been institutionalized for most of his life before moving to a group home. His antecedents to aggression were very difficult to miss. He would invariably say, "Call Security," just prior to an all-out physical aggression!

Triggers are situations, people, places, or events that directly lead to physical acting out. Examples may be the presence of a visitor to your classroom, a high demand situation for the student, or an event at home prior to the school day. It is crucial for teachers and other staff to recognize that both triggers and antecedents are likely to be present in the first stage of crisis development.

Question 19

> Name an antecedent behavior and a trigger for aggressive behavior
> that you have observed in one of your students.

_____

_____

_____

_____

_____

_____

_____

If the teacher, or others, is not able to de-escalate the student's behavior in the first stage of crisis development, the student may progress to the next stage, which is active crisis. In this stage, the teacher has made the judgment that the student is now a clear and present danger to himself, others, or property. The student's behavior has likely escalated past the point where verbal management will be effective (the student probably does not hear you anymore) and direct intervention is necessary for safety. The direct intervention itself, depending on the locale of the school and its behavior management guidelines, if any, will range from an intervention team, to a seclusion time-out, to police involvement. Whatever your situation, it is good practice to get a team on the scene as unobtrusively as possible. Try to avoid using intercoms unless you absolutely have to, as this can add abundant attention for the behavior we want to minimize attention for. When the team is on the scene, try to use physical intervention as a last resort. If you have to intervene, obey all laws, regulations, and prohibitions regarding restraints that are applicable. It is beyond the scope of this text to discuss the pros and cons of restraint, but knowing the regulations and knowing that physical intervention should always be the last resort are essential for the teacher to remember.

The crisis will end at some point and this is called the postvention stage. Typically active crisis situations last a few seconds to a few minutes as the high energy required for these behaviors is not able to be maintained much longer. You may encounter a situation in which there is some calming, then re-entering of crisis repeatedly—a "continuous crisis" with periods of calming interspersed throughout the whole time period. Regardless, once the crisis is completed, the student enters the last stage of crisis development, which is the resolution stage. The teacher's response to the resolution of the crisis is the postvention stage. In this stage, energy subsides. Sometimes the student realizes she has done something wrong, and the crisis situation is effectively over. It is desirable that some learning occur during the teacher's postvention, so the suggested protocol is to have the student go back to the routine or task. The teacher should wait 5 to 7 minutes, and then praise the student for any desirable behavior that is in evidence (e.g., sitting in seat, working). This approach teaches the student that there is no reinforcement available for crisis behaviors, but for desirable behaviors the reinforcement is abundant. One special note—teachers should be particularly careful about having students overly apologize for their misbehavior. If a student makes too many apologies, it can inadvertently reinforce the misbehavior by providing too much attention for it. If you want a student to apologize to you or others, make it very short and move on! Remember, you are trying to maximize attention for desirable behavior and minimize attention for undesirable behavior.

One of the benefits of mastering this model of crisis development is that the teacher can insert a student's behavior into the model at any given time. If she is in the antecedent/precursor stage, the teacher can try verbal management. If she is past that stage and into active crisis, the teacher must ask the following questions: What do I do for safety? Is the crisis over? What part of the routine do I have the student re-enter during postvention?

Verbal Management of Behavior and Changing the Environment

A very important field skill for teachers to have is a verbal management repertoire, which is key for crisis de-escalation. Intervening verbally with a student who is early in crisis development generally has a better prognosis than intervening verbally with a student who is nearing active crisis. There are numerous verbal management techniques available for teachers to use. Redirection is a strategy that is often used and involves the student being prompted by the teacher to relocate to a different area of the room, begin another task, and so on. It can be effective if the relocation takes the student's mind off the crisis, but it really relies on the student engaging in another task or activity in the other location. Refocusing interest is another technique that involves the teacher prompting the student to think about or discuss a favorite topic and is another form of redirection. I have used both of these techniques with great success. One individual was so interested in professional wrestling that he was able to be refocused on discussions of his favorite wrestlers. Another student was very much interested in jewelry and could be refocused fairly easily to jewelry topics.

Another technique is the use of humor, but it can also easily backfire and make a bad situation worse. The humor must always be directed toward you the teacher or someone or something else, never toward the student. Can you see that if a student's behavior is escalating and that he now perceives he is being laughed at, this perception could escalate the behavior further? However, if you can get a student laughing, who was on the verge of physically acting out, the situation may de-escalate (unless, of course, it is some type of demonic laughter).

Teachers may also choose to use problem-solving approaches to de-escalate student behavior. A common approach is to have the student attempt to solve the issue on her own or to provide help in finding the solution. An example is when a student is upset and agitated because she cannot find her lunch. The teacher could organize a search party, involve other students, or encourage the student herself to retrace her steps to try to find it. This technique often works because the student is actively working to solve the problem, with or without assistance.

Reinterpretation or clarification is another verbal de-escalation technique that involves the teacher dispelling some misconception or misperception that the student holds that is contributing to the acting out behavior. An example is a student with whom I was working who suddenly, and with no history of these types of behaviors, began aggressing toward staff, broke a television set, and pulled out some of his own hair. We finally discovered (after initially thinking it was a medical/medication issue) that this student had overheard the old saying "Only the good die young," and truly believed that he "had to be bad to live." We had to reinterpret and clarify for this young man that this was only a saying and that he was probably going to live a long, happy, and productive life. Imagine the misperceptions and misconceptions that your students may hold!

Another technique is called authoritative commands. This involves the teacher gaining control of the escalating situation by issuing a firm directive to the student in a stern, yet not loud, tone of voice. Often the teacher is able to regain some control over the situation by directing the student to a certain location, task, or activity. You must be careful with this technique, however, as it may inadvertently escalate the situation.

The last verbal management technique is called direct appeals. These may be appeals to personal improvement, undesirable/desirable consequences, or social expectations. In a direct appeal to personal improvement, the teacher intervenes by calling attention to a student's recent accomplishments, prosocial behavior, or any other pleasant things in the student's academic life. This technique often works as it refocuses the student on his recent appropriate behavior and away from crisis development. Please note that if the student has not had recent appropriate behavior or other desirable topics to discuss, do not use this technique. The teacher can also use a direct appeal to undesirable/desirable consequences, which is another technique to be very careful with! Using this approach, you simply inform the student as to what is going to happen if the escalation continues or if it ceases. The teacher could inform a student, "As soon as you are calm, we are going outside and then we will _____ later." Sometimes this technique is very effective because the student now has clear information and can make a choice. The last direct appeal is to social expectations and involves informing the student that "we do not do that here, we do _____ instead." This projects to the student that not only is the teacher expecting certain behavior, but also that many people are expecting the correct behavior (e.g., the school, the community). This technique can be very effective with students who are cognizant of the numbers of people involved, which can literally be hundreds.

Another technique available to teachers for de-escalation is extinction or planned ignoring. Using this technique with very specific students, the teacher simply ignores the escalation of behavior and waits for the student to de-escalate on his or her own. An example would be students who escalate their behavior as soon as the teacher intervenes, or students whose behavior worsens as soon as verbal intervention occurs. Some students do better at calming themselves down rather than responding to the de-escalation being initiated by the teacher or staff. One of the overall goals of behavior intervention plans should be teaching the student to manage his or her own behavior. Self-management should be taught and reinforced. While planned ignoral or extinction is occurring, it is crucial that the teacher still monitor the student's behavior for escalation or calming. Planned ignoring and extinction is another technique that could be extremely dangerous if mishandled. Can you imagine what would happen with some students if the teacher ignored the escalation? However, with a small, specific group of students, the better approach is not to attend to the antecedents and let them extinguish themselves.

There are also some techniques for crisis de-escalation that involve the environment and changes that the teacher can make in the classroom setting. Stimulation or overstimulation in the environment may be a trigger for physically acting out. The teacher can decrease stimuli or increase stimuli as a de-escalation technique. Turning off the radio, getting some students out of the room, or removing some pictures from the wall are all examples of decreasing stimuli. Conversely, the teacher can also increase stimuli for some students who are escalating due to lack of stimulation (some students may act out due to sheer boredom). Getting a student involved in the routine, a task, an errand, and so on, are all examples of increasing stimuli. An actual change in environment is also a technique based on the realization that some acting out behavior is inappropriate only because of where it is occurring. In other words, running around in circles, yelling, and throwing yourself on the floor is certainly considered inappropriate in a classroom, but is it more acceptable in the gym? on the playground outside? Teachers can either relocate the student to the new environment, or they may choose to convert a part of their classroom to a "mini-gym" where they have mats, equipment, and so on, and can instantly put the student in that part of their room to accommodate the behavior.

Teachers now have 13 verbal and environmental de-escalation techniques to use in the classroom, and it is very important to use them as early as possible in crisis development.

Question 20

Name and define three verbal de-escalation techniques, and explain how you might use each in your classroom.

a. _____

_____

_____

_____

b. _____

_____

_____

_____

c. _____

_____

_____

_____

Dressing for Safety

It is apparent that the classroom should be safe and that students should feel safe and secure while with the teacher. Teachers can examine their environment and check for possible weapons (there are usually at least a couple of objects that could be used as weapons), and also for breakable items that could injure others. As teachers examine their classrooms, they may find that some materials are safer than others, that is, teachers may decide to remove all glass objects, to not have as many personal effects on their desk, to move activities away from the windows, or to use wood blocks instead of plastic, breakable ones.

After the teacher has examined the classroom environment, the next step is to examine how the teacher should dress for a typical school day and critique typical daily dress for safety. Teachers should avoid large hoop earrings, open-toed footwear, long flowing hairstyles, and long, flowing dresses. Dressing for safety involves keeping the teacher safe by minimizing the number of "grab holds" that a student could use during a physical aggression. Common sense goes a long way in this area.

Stress Management for Teachers

To those who teach students who exhibit aggressive or destructive behavior, first of all, Bless You! You have a very difficult job and may be experiencing some stress as a result of your career choice. Teachers experience stress for many reasons, among them student behavior, administrative issues, burdensome paperwork, peer conflict, personal life issues, money and bills, and some atypical stressors. Teaching is a stressful occupation that is compounded when you teach students who engage in health- or life-threatening behaviors such as physical aggression or property destruction.

The last field skill addressed is teacher stress management. This is another crucial skill for a teacher's behavioral repertoire because stress can hurt or even kill an individual. Stress is highly ranked as a risk factor for heart disease, and some teachers report somatic complaints related to stress such as back or chest pain, digestive disorders, or headaches. If teachers do not have at least a few stress management techniques that work for them, stress is very likely to haunt them.

Part of stress management is analyzing what is stressing the teacher and recognizing that much of the stress that we all experience is self-induced. We do it to ourselves! Obviously, it is typically people, places, things, situations, or events that stress teachers out. But too often, it is not the person, place, thing, situation, or event that is really stressing the teacher out. It is the teacher's perception of it. We all have stress perceptions. A common one for teachers is "awfulizing," which is a tendency to see things as being 100 times worse than they really are. Another is "demandedness," which is having to have things our way or else, and judgementalism, which is making snap judgments about people, places, things, and so on. There is also the "everything has to run smoothly" syndrome wherein teachers believe that there should never be any problems of any kind in their classroom, including behavior problems. Sometimes if the teacher changes her perception of the person, or event, and so on, she can reduce stress immediately. It is like "getting your head together" and your body will follow. A decent mindset for teachers to have is "that you might encounter some behavior problems today, but you will prevent most of them and safely handle those that you cannot prevent."

Two specific stress management techniques, or stress reactive strategies, are a sense of humor and variety versus the "rut." A good sense of humor can be a nice counterbalance to stress, and teachers have to admit that some things that happen in the classroom are funny. They may not be very funny while they are happening, but teachers can certainly enjoy a chuckle about them later. Seeing the humor in some situations can go a long way toward reducing stress that can be caused by taking things too seriously sometimes. Every once in a while, everyone needs to get out of a rut and experience something new or change how they do things. Try a new route to work, go to a show or restaurant you have never been to before, or use Visa to pay Mastercard. Just "shake things up a bit," and it can really help.

Other techniques include "venting" either physically or verbally. Some teachers excel at releasing pent-up stress by letting it all out verbally to a friend or coprofessional. Other teachers vent physically via exercise, organized sports, low impact exercises like walks, or more high impact exercises like martial arts. There are many individualized techniques for stress management that teachers have developed including shopping sprees, alone time, and meditation. Some teachers find their greatest stress reliever is their faith. However you choose to do it, it can be quite cathartic to vent your stress.

As a teacher you must find a technique or combination of techniques that work for you and use them on a consistent basis to prevent and relieve stress. Do not let stress haunt you!

Question 21

You currently have high stress levels. Offer three stressors that may have created this stress and three stress management techniques that you could use to decrease your stress level.

a. _____

_____

_____

_____

b. _____

_____

_____

_____

c. _____

_____

_____

_____

_____

In closing, remember two things. First, students may forget what you say; they may even forget what you do, but they will never forget how you made them feel. It makes sense to me that we should be making students feel good about themselves to the best of our ability, and that the better students feel about themselves the less likely they are to engage in aggressive behavior. Second, in the end, it does not matter how many crises you manage. It matters how many you prevent.

FINAL EXAMINATION

1. Target a behavior for change in your classroom, and give a rationale for the behavior you have chosen being at least desirable and necessary to change.

    _____

    _____

    _____

    _____

    _____

    _____

2. Operationally define physical aggression or property destruction for one of your students.

    _____

    _____

    _____

    _____

    _____

3. Is your operational definition IBSOM? Would you be able to collect data using this definition?

    _____

    _____

    _____

    _____

    _____

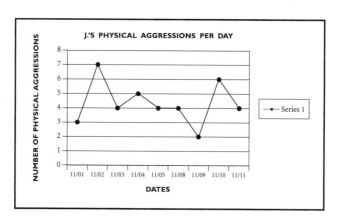

Use the graph above for questions 4 through 7.

4. Is this baseline stable, variable, ascending, or descending?

    _____

5. Is there any trend in evidence?

    _____

6. What is the average number of aggressions per day for student J.?

    _____

7. What are your reflections on this baseline?

    _____

    _____

    _____

    _____

    _____

    _____

    _____

    _____

8. What would you do if program drift became evident in your classroom with a new behavior intervention program? What could you do immediately to prevent program anarchy?

_____

_____

_____

_____

_____

_____

_____

_____

_____

_____

9. Name three forms of current data collection in your classroom and explain how they are used. If you do not currently collect behavior data, suggest three forms that might work for you.

   a. _____

   _____

   _____

   b. _____

   _____

   _____

   c. _____

   _____

   _____

10. Ariel, a student in your classroom, has been presenting aggressive behavior in the form of punching classmates with a closed fist with moderate force. She averages 4.5 incidents per school day, and the new behavior intervention program has reduced this rate to an average of 2.0 incidents per school day after a full week of implementation. Is your program a success? Why or why not? What other information do you need to decide?

_____

_____

_____

_____

_____

_____

_____

_____

11. For one of your students, identify one thing that seems to make his or her aggressive behavior happen in the classroom and one thing that seems to keep the behavior happening.

_____

_____

_____

_____

12. Critique your classroom in terms of entry point #1. What areas do you see as strengths? What areas need improvement, and how will you improve them?

_____

_____

_____

_____

_____

_____

_____

_____

_____

13. For one of your students who engages in aggressive or destructive behavior, name an approach for each entry point for behavior change that you could incorporate in your classroom.

_____

_____

_____

_____

_____

_____

_____

_____

_____

_____

14. How does your classroom affect student behavior? Name three specific ways in which a classroom can increase or decrease aggressive student behavior.

   a. _____

   _____

   _____

b. _____

_____

_____

c. _____

_____

_____

15. Name a functional alternative for a student who is chronically hitting his teacher to get his or her attention. How would you go about teaching this new behavior?

_____

_____

_____

_____

_____

_____

_____

_____

_____

_____

16. Suggest an alternative response, and explain how you would teach this alternative response for the following behaviors of concern.

a. Student hits peers to gain their attention.

_____

_____

_____

_____

b. Student is aggressive toward you to gain your attention or to escape.

_____

_____

_____

_____

c. Student destroys property and seems to be maintained by attention and the sound of the objects breaking.

_____

_____

_____

_____

17. Name three behaviors in your classroom that you would praise and why you would praise these behaviors.

a. _____

_____

_____

_____

b. _____

_____

_____

_____

c. _____

_____

_____

_____

18. Name an alternative behavior for physical aggression or property destruction that you could teach a student, and write a behavior contract for the new behavior.

   _____

   _____

   _____

   _____

   _____

   _____

   _____

   _____

   _____

   _____

19. Name an antecedent behavior and a trigger for aggressive behavior that you have observed in one of your students.

   _____

   _____

   _____

   _____

   _____

20. Name and define three verbal de-escalation techniques, and explain how you might use each in your classroom.

   a. _____

   _____

   _____

   _____

b. _____

_____

_____

_____

c. _____

_____

_____

_____

21. You currently have high stress levels. Offer three stressors that may have created this stress and three stress management techniques that you could use to decrease your stress level.

a. _____

_____

_____

_____

b. _____

_____

_____

_____

c. _____

_____

_____

_____

ANSWER KEY

1. Behaviors selected will vary, but answers must include justification for selecting behavior. Answers should mention health-threatening, life-threatening behavior and danger to student and others.

2. Answers must include specific actions that make up the aggressive or destructive behavior, and the operational definition must be specific, observable, and measurable.

3. Answers will vary.

4. The baseline is variable.

5. There is no trend because there are not three consecutive data points heading in the same direction.

6. J. averages 4.33 physical aggressions per school day.

7. Answers will vary, but should include mention of the variability of the baseline and that there seems to be no trend.

8. Answers should mention retraining of staff and all persons involved with the student and close monitoring of the behavior intervention plan to prevent future drift or anarchy.

9. Answers will vary.

10. Answers should include the need for more time to see if decreases in aggression or destruction are sustained. Also answers should mention the need for more information on behavior, for example, duration of episodes, as the rate may have decreased, but the duration may have increased.

11. Answers will vary.

12. Answers will vary.

13. Answers must include an intervention for each entry point #1 through #4.

14. Answers must mention level of stimulation, temperature, classroom rules, and other entry point #1 considerations.

15. Answers must include a functional alternative such as communication, and a method for teaching it such as behavior contracts, modeling, or the like.

16. Same as question 15 for all three scenarios.

17. Behaviors selected should be prosocial, cooperative, adaptive responses such as hand raising, correct academic responding, and so on, and a justification given as to why the teacher would like to see more of these behaviors in the future.

18. Alternative behaviors such as communication, coping skills, and so on, should be included as well as a contract specified in "I, _____ agree to do _____, in order to get _____" terms.

19. Answers will vary.

20. Answers must include specific techniques from the text such as redirection, refocusing interest, direct appeals, and so on, and the applications must occur in the antecedent stage of crisis development, before active crisis.

21. Stressors will vary; stress management techniques may include venting, changing stress perceptions, and so on.

REFERENCES AND FURTHER READINGS

Alberto, P. A., & Troutman, A. C. (1999). *Applied behavior analysis for teachers.* Upper Saddle River, NJ: Merrill.

Allison, G. S. (1987, April). A direct service delivery approach to crisis prevention. *CPI National Report, III,* 23–28.

Allison, G. S. (1989, February). Innovative techniques in crisis prevention. *CPI National Report, IV,* 8–11.

Fagan, J. (1996). Recent perspectives on youth violence. Paper presented at the Northwest Conference on Youth Violence, Seattle, WA.

Goldstein, A. P., Palumbo, J., Striepling, S., & Voutsinas, A. M. (1995). *Break it up: A teacher's guide to managing student aggression.* Champaign, IL: Research Press.

Larson, J. (1998). Managing student aggression in high schools: Implications for practice. *Psychology in the Schools, 35,* 283–291.

Leff, S. S., Power, T. J., & Manz, P. H. (2001). School-based aggression prevention programs for young children: Current status and implications for violence prevention. *Journal of School Psychology, 30,* 344–382.

Loeber, R., & Farrington, D. P. (1998). *Serious and violent juvenile offenders: Risk factors and successful interventions.* Thousand Oaks, CA: Sage.

Sprague, J., & Walker, H. (2000). Early identification and intervention for youth with antisocial and violent behavior. *Exceptional Children, 66,* 3, 367–379.

Wehby, J. H. (1994). Issues in the assessment of aggressive behavior. *Preventing School Failure, 38,* 24–28.

Zirpoli, T. J., & Melloy, K. J. (1997). *Behavior management: Applications for teachers and parents.* Upper Saddle River, NJ: Merrill.

Related Web Sites

www.guidancechannel.com—articles and information on school violence, conflict resolution, and more

www.newcentsol.com—three steps to prevent school violence, how to make school safer for students and faculty

www.youthchg.com—the problem kid problem solver site, live features help to answer questions

www.judge-for-yourself.com—a clearinghouse site for all major sites that specialize in school violence

ABOUT THE AUTHOR

Gary Stephen Allison is assistant professor of special education at the University of Delaware. He received his doctorate from Wilmington College and has been working with students with severe/profound disabilities and exceptional behavior challenges for over 30 years. Dr. Allison serves on the professional advisory board of the Epilepsy Foundation of Delaware and has received numerous awards for service and excellence in teaching at the undergraduate and graduate levels. His areas of interest include treatment of health- and life-threatening behavior in students with severe/profound disabilities, inclusion and access to meaningful educational opportunities for students with severe/profound disabilities, and the professional preparation and development of teachers in special education.

Credit Card/PO Billing Address

Name _____

Address _____

_____

_____

Ship To: Telephone Number _____

Name _____

Address _____

_____

_____

GUARANTEE

All products are sold on 30-day approval. If you are not satisfied, you can return any product within 30 days. Please contact our office to receive authorization and necessary shipping instructions for returns. Prepaid orders will receive prompt refund, less handling charges. **Please use our fax number (1-800-FXPROED or 1-800/397-7633)!**

PAYMENT: All orders must be prepaid in full in U.S. funds by check or money order payable to PRO-ED, Inc., or by credit card. Open accounts are available to book-stores, public schools, libraries, institutions, and corporations. Please prepay first order and send full credit information to open an account.

Billing Authorization (must be completed or we cannot bill)

Purchase Order Number _____

❏ **Payment Enclosed**

Credit Card ❏ VISA ❏ MasterCard ❏ AMEX ❏ Discover

NOTE: Credit card billing address at top left must be completed if your order is charged to a credit card.

Authorized Signature _____

Card Number _____

Expiration Date _____

If prices on your order are incorrect, we reserve the right to exceed the amount up to 10% unless otherwise stated on your order. Terms are net, F.O.B. Austin, Texas; prices are subject to change without notice. ALL ORDERS MUST BE PAID IN U.S. FUNDS.

Quantity	Prod. No.	Book Title	Unit Price	Total
	10467	*How To Help Students Remain Seated*	$ 9.00	
	10468	*How To Deal Effectively with Lying, Stealing, and Cheating*	$ 9.00	
	10469	*How To Prevent and Safely Manage Physical Aggression and Property Destruction*	$ 9.00	
	10470	*How To Help Students Complete Classwork and Homework Assignments*	$ 9.00	
	10471	*How To Help Students Play and Work Together*	$ 9.00	
	10472	*How To Deal with Students Who Challenge and Defy Authority*	$ 9.00	
	10473	*How To Deal Effectively with Whining and Tantrum Behaviors*	$ 9.00	
	10474	*How To Help Students Follow Directions, Pay Attention, and Stay on Task*	$ 9.00	
	10465	All 8 *How To* titles	$56.00	

Product Total _____

Handling, Postage, and Carrying Charges
(U.S. add 10%; Canada add 15%; others add 20%. Minimum charge $1.00) _____

Subtotal _____

Texas residents ONLY add 8.25% sales tax or WRITE IN TAX-EXEMPT NUMBER _____

Grand Total (U.S. Funds Only) _____

NOTES

NOTES

NOTES

NOTES